Santa Takes a Tumble

Other books by Len Boswell

A Grave Misunderstanding
Flicker: A Paranormal Mystery
Skeleton: A Bare Bones Mystery
The Leadership Secrets of Squirrels

Santa Takes a Tumble

12 Days of Christmas Past for "Kids" Beyond Belief

Len Boswell

This is a work of creative nonfiction. I have tried to recreate events, locales and conversations from my memories of them. In order to maintain their anonymity, in some instances I have changed the names of individuals and places. I also may have changed some identifying characteristics and details such as physical properties, occupations and places of residence. Santa Claus, of course, plays himself throughout.

To all I love without condition
To all I love without omission

Never doubt

"One Christmas was so much like another, in those years around the sea-town corner now and out of all sound except the distant speaking of the voices I sometimes hear a moment before sleep, that I can never remember whether it snowed for six days and six nights when I was twelve or whether it snowed for twelve days and twelve nights when I was six."

— Dylan Thomas, *A Child's Christmas in Wales*

"A lovely thing about Christmas is that it's compulsory, like a thunderstorm, and we all go through it together."

–Garrison Keillor, *Leaving Home*

"Happy, happy Christmas, that can win us back to the delusions of our childish days; that can recall to the old man the pleasures of his youth . . .

–Charles Dickens, *The Pickwick Papers*

Contents

Preface

YOU MAY NOT BELIEVE IN SANTA CLAUS, at least not at your current age, but if you celebrate Christmas, you know there was a time when you believed with all your heart, a time when you weren't quite sure, and a time when the truth became all too clear. The twelve stories that follow reflect a mix of those emotions and events, told by the man — then boy — who experienced them in the early 1950s.

As anyone who has experienced Christmas morning can tell you, there will be joy and pain, disappointment and even heartbreak — the whole panoply of emotions on proud and not-so-proud display. Most of the stories are funny, and some are poignant; all are meant to remind you of your own stories of those halcyon days, when you laid in bed with tooth-picked eyes, trying with all your might to stay awake long enough to see the jolly old elf.

— LEN BOSWELL

AND SO WE BEGIN . . .

I am eight again, tugging on shoes too small and holey mittens warmed overnight on the living room radiator. I have already donned two pairs of pants and my only three shirts to brace myself against the cold. My mother appears beside me, young and pretty as always, insisting that I wear my Christmas scarf, a scratchy abomination as long as an anaconda, knitted loosely and tightly by my Aunt Louise, using a geometry known only to her. Despite my protests, she wraps Scarf Louisienne around my neck several times and nudges me toward the front door.

Outside, the world is white and still, the only sound the whisper of the falling snow. I lift my head to the snowy heavens, stick out my tongue, and accept winter's cold communion.

Come, we have much to see.

Day 1

OH, CHRISTMAS TREE!

EVERY FAMILY HAS ITS OWN UNIQUE TRADITIONS when it comes to Christmas trees, and it was no different when I was growing up. Mrs. Peeps, who lived directly across the street from us, always had a blue spruce just tall enough for her knitted white angel to forever bend at the waist, its head and back scraping the ceiling. There were no ornaments on her tree, also a tradition, and only blue lights. The Armisters, our better-off friends, preferred artificial, flocked-white trees, with white ornaments, and white lights, for their pale homage to Christmas. That's just how they rolled.

And then there was our tree.

Shaggy, gangly, too tall, too wide, of suspect species, our tree stood, leaned, or floated in the corner of our living room, held in place by defective tree stands and poorly engineered guywires to create a state of tenuous stability. And yes, I said floated. That was the year our tree stand died, and my father came up with the brilliant plan of suspending the tree from the ceiling, which had the novel effect of making the tree rotate, first to the right, until the rope knotted tight, and then back to the left, gathering speed as it turned, a victim of whatever air currents were handy.

I remember our cat Sylvester watching the rotating tree intently, one paw raised, ready to bat at the swirling ornaments, then running for cover when the tree reversed direction and headed back his way.

Ah, the ornaments.

If you could make them, we had them: paper chains, strung popcorn, cutout cardboard figures of gingerbread men or angels or steam locomotives — anything our scissors imagined. Real candy canes and cookies baked with string loops were also a must, and provided our first meal on Christmas morning.

Did you have glass ornaments?

Yes, a few, and none the same, and most collected from yard sales by my father, who had a deft eye for disturbingly grim ornaments, particularly glass Santas that looked more like gargoyles than jolly old elves, or large globe ornaments of a color reminiscent of the La Brea Tar Pits.

What about lights?

Oh, we had them, at least for those brief hours when all the bulbs functioned properly. Nothing as fancy as the Armister's lights, those bubbling candle lights that forever bubble in my memory as Mrs. Armister, thin as a pin, puts another paper roll in their player piano, which did its best to play a few carols as we sipped hot chocolate from tiny china cups. No, we just had standard lights of all colors. My father would start at the bottom of the tree and make a spiral of lights as he worked his way to the top. If he had planned correctly, the last light would glow at the top of the tree. Some years, it was the middle of the tree, though. And one year, he had a clump of lights left when he reached the top, so he just hung the clump at the top. My father believed in kismet when it came to Christmas tree lights—wherever they ended up, they ended up, and far be it from him or anyone else to change that. It was just part of the ineffable magic of Christmas.

Did you put tinsel on the tree?
We called them icicles, and they were made of thin strips of aluminum foil, and it was the job of me, my brother, and my sister to put them on the tree. My sister preferred to separate the icicles into separate strands, then consider each strand's proper place on the tree, then place the strands just so, so that the draped icicle was of equal lengths on both sides. My brother and I opted for rapid deployment of the icicles, tossing them by the handful at the tree, from various angles and distances, in more of an "icicles happen" approach. Any that fell to the floor during this process would be scooped up, along with dust and cat hair, and be tossed at the tree again, until the tree was loaded. Then one of us would climb the open stairs behind the tree and top it off with our one-winged angel, Gladys. And then the tree would be officially complete.

Some years the tree was perfect and magical. Other years the tree look cluttered or sparse, or seemed to be the victim of gale winds, ornaments akimbo, blown to one side. And in still other years, the tree resembled an old man weighted down by layer after layer of colorful rags. But they were our trees, and we loved them all.

When did you put up your tree?
Always on Christmas Eve, which is when we'd either

buy a tree, at a greatly reduced price, or cut down a tree in the woods at the bottom of our street, although that sometimes meant tying several small scraggily trees together to create a bushier tree.

And how long did you leave your tree up?
The tree went up on Christmas Eve and came down on New Year's Eve, according to my mother's wishes and deep superstitions. She thought it was bad luck to have two Christmas trees in the same year. Besides, with trees so beautiful, so magnificent, so magical, who could bear such intense orgasmic joy for more than a week?

Day 2
A CHRISTMAS TOTEM

I CAN STILL SEE THE THIN LAYER OF SNOW and hear it crunch under the soles of my Roy Rogers galoshes as my father and I crouch-walked through the woods in search of a Christmas tree. It was Christmas Eve and, unlike previous eves, when we invariably picked up our tree for next to nothing, or nothing at all, at a nearby Boy Scouts lot, this Christmas Eve had not gone well. The lot had been picked clean of all but a few handfuls of pine needles, and the boy scouts were tearing down their camp and dousing the fire that had warmed them the last few weeks.

Not to be deterred, my father had come up with a Plan B, prefaced with a string of obscenities aimed at no one in particular. Finally, he had shouted, "We'll cut down our own damn tree," his voice rising, the force of "damn tree" causing the scouts to back off and scatter. In my memory, I clearly recall one of them shouting for a "Mr. Beasly," no doubt the scoutmaster, but Mr. Beasly was nowhere in evidence, so the boy had stood there, flapping his arms and shouting, "Oh, shit, oh shit!"

And with that we returned home to collect a saw and flashlights before trudging down the hill to the woods that marked the end of civilization.

We trudged. And we trudged, the cold insinuating itself into my galoshes, through the barrier of newspaper I had wrapped around my feet for warmth, into my ankles, spreading up to my knees, at which point, in frustration, I laid my first F-bomb on my dad, urging him to quit the search.

He just stared at me blankly, as if the F-bomb could not possibly have come from my lips, then grunted, picked out three scrub pines at random, not a one with a trunk thicker than a big toe, and sawed them down.

"We'll make do," he said.

I started to protest, but the cold had crept up my thighs and was threatening to reach higher, so I just nodded, grabbed hold of one of the little trees, and started dragging it toward home, not even looking back to make sure my dad was still with me.

Once there, I dropped the little tree outside and raced into the house, which had the welcome warmth of a blast furnace. As I recuperated in the kitchen with cocoa and over-baked sugar cookies, I could hear my father dragging the trees inside to the protests of my older sister — "that's not a tree!" — and the bawling of my younger brother, who was given to tears several times a day back then, often without reason.

"Well, it's not a tree now, but it will be," my father said.

And it was, in a way, although not in any way that would suggest "Christmas Tree." Tied together with twine, the "tree" was more like a piney bush, as wide as it was tall, with limbs shooting this way and that, but not in any way that would suggest the work of nature. Not even Charlie Brown could have imagined such an abomination.

My mother laughed at the tree every time she looked

at it, but then, she was that kind of woman, laughter being her antidote in times of stress and hardship, which was always. I and my brother and sister had a different response, which could euphemistically be called "grumbling," mostly under our breath, for fear our father would hear us.

Trimming the tree made matters worse. Loaded down with tinsel, it looked like some shaggy, tinseled yak. That's when my brother began to cry again, inconsolably, drawing the attention of my mother, who came into the room, took one look at the newly decorated tree, and actually went beyond a laugh, even beyond a guffaw, to some unnamed form of laughter that could only be the stuff of legend.

And that's when things went terribly wrong. My father — let me be kind — lost it, rushing into the room, grabbing the fully decorated tree, and throwing it out the front door and down the steps, where it would remain until Easter as a cautionary totem for our neighbors in general and our postman in particular, his pace quickening as he walked up to the mailbox, deposited the mail, and fled.

In his defense, my father claimed that his actions were not only unavoidable, but justifiable, because we didn't have the Christmas spirit, although those were not his exact words. And perhaps we didn't.

And yet, whenever I think of a heavily tinseled yak, I invariably think of Christmas.

Day 3
ESCAPE VELOCITY

THERE WERE SO MANY SNOWS in the winters of my youth, but few on Christmas Day. Weather forecasting was more a combination of art and Ouija Board back then, and it would be years before the science of meteorology surpassed the uncanny accuracy of a Magic 8 Ball. So every morning held the promise of magic, and disappointment.

On this particular morning, a week before Christmas, Frosty the Snowman, who was clearly in my pantheon of Norse gods, came through, bringing forth a storm not so much remembered for its depth, but for its quality, each flake conspiring to couple with its fellow flakes to create the slickest surface possible for a sled.

In those days, sleds were pretty much it. Occasionally, you would see someone on wooden skis, usually some old man wearing ear muffs and an overly long scarf, puffing on a pipe while struggling to maintain his balance with every faltering glide, but there were no snowboards to be had, and we would have thought the concept insane in any case. Balance yourself on a board? Are you out of your mind? Why would anyone want anything but a sled, preferably a Flexible Flyer, although Comets and Lightning Gliders had their charms?

My routine on "sledding days" was always the same. I would race to the basement and wrestle my way through stacks of boxes to uncover my sled, a Flexible Flyer that was old and beat up when I got it, and warped somewhat, the sled much preferring to go left rather than straight. It was so old and worn that even its once proud name had been worn down to "ex Fly."

Once I'd found the sled, I had to check the runners for rust, which I would scrape off with one of my father's collection of rusty files, or if things weren't too bad, a sheet of sandpaper wrapped around a block of wood. If I had been more scientific about it, I guess I would have added some exotic wax to increase my speed, but given the severe incline of our sledding hill, attaining speed was never a problem.

Clothing was as important as the sled, of course, but these were the days when cotton and wool were king, so there would be no miracle fabrics to insulate me from the cold or keep me dry. First came pajama bottoms, then jeans, then corduroy pants, which swished musically with every step. Three pairs of socks, galoshes, a scarf, a wool cap, three or more shirts or sweaters, a coat, and mittens completed the ensemble.

And then I was out the door, dragging my sled down R Street to the corner, where I took a right onto Arcadia Avenue. The neighborhood was easy to navigate back then. It was a simple grid of avenues and lettered streets. Walking down Arcadia, I would encounter S Street, then T, then U, then V, then W, and then, inexplicably, Alton Street, my ultimate destination. Every street has its memories. Mimi Shelton lived at the corner of R and Arcadia. She was said to have been born in the family toilet. In my memory, she is a frail girl in pigtails, a finger forever up her nose.

A little ways up Arcadia, just before S Street, I'd pass four landmarks: the home of my friends, the Benedettis (Tony, Luigi, and Boo-Boo); the empty lot where we played tackle football without helmets or other equipment, and dreamed of being Redskins quarterback Eddie LaBaron; the very spot where my brother was bitten in the face by the Benedetti's German Shepherd, Moose, leaving a scar over his right eye that spelled "OK"; and the intersection of Arcadia with S Street, where I saw my neighbor, Alex Crumb, get hit by a car, leaving him alive, but with uncontrollable jerks and spasms that affected him the rest of his life.

As I crossed that intersection, the road began to dip down dramatically, growing steeper and steeper as Arcadia Avenue passed over T Street, then bottomed out at U Street, which was aptly named. If you stood in the intersection of U and Arcadia and looked back toward R, then turned and looked the other direction, up toward V and W and Alton, you would have the feeling that you were standing at the bottom of a giant letter U. And that was the course I would be sledding, starting at the peak of Alton street, racing down Arcadia past W and V, and bottoming out at U, my sled slowing to a stop well before I reached T. Or at least that was the plan.

By the time I huffed and puffed my way up to Alton, the hill was alive with dozens of kids of all sizes and ages, from toddlers to fuzzy-chinned teens. The boy in me has to admit that there were "even girls" there, including Betty Sue Whipple, the heart throb of every 12-year-old boy in the neighborhood, including me. She was holding court in her pink furry boots at the top of the hill, waving off every request by boys eager to double up with her on a sled.

My first run was faster than I expected, forcing me to drag my feet to prevent jackknifing at the bottom. Everyone seemed to be having the same problem, so someone had the bright idea to build a ramp at the bottom of U Street, an incline cobbled together out of snow and tree limbs and broken down apple crates, to help with the transition up toward T Street.

It worked beautifully the first few runs, the sleds speeding up the ramp and going airborne for twenty feet or more before landing smoothly on the incline from U to T. But then the course became too fast, too icy, the speeds so great that kids and sleds flew separate ways when they hit the ramp. A few of the kids decided to call it a day, and head on home, but most of us stayed, standing in small groups at the top of the hill, discussing how to deal with the speed of the course. I think it was Tony Benedetti who suggested we try doubling and tripling up on the sleds, either sitting or lying down — "pancaking" — as a way to reduce the speeds. Everyone thought that was a good idea, except Betty Sue, who waggled a finger at us and said, "No, no, no."

It didn't work. The course was still too fast. We should have just gone home, but then someone had the "brilliant" idea to use something other than a sled to go down the course. It was an idea that had come up before, in previous snows, as we stood at the corner of Alton and Arcadia, where Jake Lombardo lived, his yard filled with his father's junked cars, whole and in pieces. The abandoned hood of an old Hudson Hornet had caught our attention more than once.

Most of us thought the idea was ridiculous. The long black hood looked more like the abandoned half-shell of a giant mussel than anything that could approximate a sled. But then Betty Sue said we could pretend it was Santa's sleigh, and she would be Mrs. Claus and the rest of us could be elves.

And so, in an act of hormone-induced insanity, we all dragged the "sleigh" to the starting line, and climbed aboard. It started off slowly, as you might expect, but then the hood and the ice formed an alliance of headlong speed, and we found ourselves hurtling down the course faster than any sled could go, terror building in us, all of us screaming.

The imagination is a wonderful thing, so I will leave it to you to describe what happened next, when the hood hit the ramp and all of us experienced the magic of flight and the certainties of gravity.

Day 4
A CHRISTMAS MASHUP

THE TABLE WAS SET, LIKE IT IS NOW, but this was years and years ago. My mother was rushing back and forth from the kitchen to the dining room with platters and bowls of food. Not in abundance, mind, because if we were in the middle class at all, we were there just recently, and barely.

The fact was my father, a self-employed upholsterer, had just delivered a sofa and two chairs back to a customer, who had paid in cash, making Christmas dinner not only possible, but a feast by our standards, which meant a meat other than price-reduced hotdogs would be involved. Our typical meal of beans on Wonder Bread, or sometimes Wonder Bread on top of beans, would be replaced by a fine ham, fresh green beans, apple sauce, mashed potatoes, and fresh-baked biscuits. There was even a rumor of pumpkin pie.

Let me be clear from the start. Meals in our home were always a matter of competition. The faster you got to the table and the faster you ate, the more likely you would be to get the calories you needed to make it till the next morning. Some people we knew actually dined, taking a leisurely approach to meals. We fed. Quickly, ravenously, covetously. My mother, rightly, thought we'd all make fine zoo animals.

My brother and I were the chief competitors, and had perfected the fine art of grab, snatch, and gobble, which invariably left my older sister sitting in front of a plate with a single slice of bread on it, and nothing more.

Needless to say, the prospect of such a glorious meal was weighing heavily on me and my brother as we sat in the living room, waiting to be called to the table. If you had seen us then, you would have sworn that we were deep in thought, dealing with a problem in astrophysics, but we were actually formulating our plan of attack. Should the ham slices be grabbed with our hands or speared with a fork? Should we use one hand or two to grab the biscuits? Would dumping the entire bowl of green beans on our plate be appropriate? Did we care?

Countermeasures were also in play. When I'm called to the table, should I throw a body block at my brother, or perhaps throw his chair away from the table, leaving him to compete for the spoils standing up? Should I create a diversion, say, throwing his Lincoln Logs across the living room?

All this, and more, was on our minds as we sat on the couch, poised for our assault, our finely honed feeding reflexes at the ready. There was one concern, though. There was a rule, a rule we dared not disobey, and that was never to attack the food before our father had loaded his plate. I think he enjoyed the game as much as we did, or so we thought, because he would sometimes load his plate slowly, holding the final spoonful over his plate for several seconds, looking back and forth at us, before depositing the food on his plate and saying, "There," which was our signal to commence our feeding frenzy.

Call it fate, call it providence, call it whatever you like, all our battle plans went out the window when our cat,

Sylvester, chose the moment we were called to dinner to launch his own attack, on our Christmas tree, racing up the trunk and grabbing my mother's handmade silk angel with his teeth, toppling the tree on his way down.

My father, mother, and sister ran for the living room to give chase. My brother and I, on the other hand, had worked ourselves into such a fine state of dinner readiness that we launched ourselves at the table, grabbing food left and right, stuffing it into our faces. By the time the rest of the family appeared, there was not much to see but culinary devastation.

Incensed, my father picked up the half-empty bowl of mashed potatoes and threw it up against the far wall of the dining room, shattering it into a million pieces and leaving a distinctive splat of mashed potatoes behind. Guilty as charged, my brother and I were summarily sent to the upstairs bedroom we shared, where we were imprisoned until morning. Our thought process back then was not so much that we were being punished, but that we were being punished before dessert. I think my brother even said, "Wait, you mean without pie?"

As wrong as we had been, my mother refused to forgive my father for throwing the mashed potatoes against the wall, destroying her one piece of good china. He, in turn, refused to clean it up, so the splat remained as a symbol of greed and pride and obstinacy for us all. And so it stayed, year after year, growing crustier with age, like each of us.

When we sold the house fifty years later, after my mother's death, the mashed potatoes were still there, a yellowed crusty splat on the dining room wall. The buyer thought the splat looked like the kind of lichens you'd see on a rotting tree stump.

Back then, though, when we were young boys, my brother thought the splat looked like a flattened reindeer. My sister, the peacemaker, who sought to mollify us all, was adamant that it looked like nothing other than a large wonderful snowflake. My father, when asked, would just look away or rattle his newspaper in front of his face. My mother would just say, "Don't get me started."

To me, it looked like the kind of splat I'd see when my snowball missed Percy Williams and hit the brick wall he was hiding behind. But now, when I think about it, I see that little splat of mashed potatoes as a symbol for each of us, all of us, a mashup of what it sometimes means to be a family just trying to make it through to the next day, moving forward from one Christmas to the next, ever struggling, ever dreaming, never more than a splat away from who knows what.

Now, could someone please pass the mashed potatoes?

Day 5
THE MAGIC CHRISTMAS PIE

THERE WERE ALWAYS CERTAIN GIVENS when it came to Christmas, and one was food, and the best was pie. Desserts were a rare thing when I was growing up. There would be the occasional pound cake now and then, or a box of donuts would suddenly appear after my mother uncharacteristically splurged at Safeway, but for the most part, desserts were restricted to Thanksgiving and Christmas.

My mother was not the best cook, and would have been the first to support a Nobel Prize for the person who invented canned food, but she could make pie, particularly pumpkin pie. It was a given, one that helped ease the pain of the wrong present or too few presents as the cloud of gift wrap and ribbons settled to the floor on Christmas morning.

My mother would see the disappointment in our faces and jump up from her chair, still in her bathrobe, and proclaim, "Time to bake pie!" Those four words eased us through the rest of the day and gave us something to look forward to as the sun set on another Christmas.

While my mother worked away in the kitchen, we played with our new toys, roamed the neighborhood looking for friends, or sat in rapt silence listening to "The Adventures of Sam Spade" on the family radio, which was taller than I was and smelled of burning wires. We were still a year away from the sci-fi wonder of our first television, a Magnavox with an eight-inch screen, which would come with a magnifying glass that would create the impression that you owned an eleven-inch screen, all the better to see the misadventures of Lucille Ball on "I Love Lucy."

From time to time, one of us would check on our mother's progress. She was not just making pie, but an entire Christmas dinner, including green beans, sweet potatoes, and one of her rare, non-canned specialties: chicken and dumplings. My mother was not one to ask for help in the kitchen, so the scene was always a bit chaotic, with pots bubbling on the stove, counters filled with utensils and food scraps, several pie pans, including one filled with fresh-plucked chicken bones, and myriad pots and pans soaking in the sudsy water of the sink. In the middle of all this was my mother, her face flush from the heat, sweat beading on her forehead. She seemed to be in six places at once, stirring, slicing, sniffing, tasting, and checking timers in a fever of what we would call multitasking today. Back then, we called it "mom."

Her one instruction to anyone who dared venture into the kitchen — her kitchen — during this time came with an outstretched arm, one finger pointing to the exit: "Go!" If she were less harried and more forgiving of your intrusion, the "go" would be preceded by a dollop of suds plopped impishly on your nose. In either case, retreat was the only option.

Finally, everything seemed to come together, and we were called to the table. Everything was wonderful, but as we sat there, stuffing our faces with chicken and dumplings, each of us kept an acquisitive eye on my mother's sewing machine, which sat in a corner of the dining room and served as a staging place for the now-cooling pumpkin pie. After a time, the clicking and clacking of forks and spoons subsided, and we all looked eagerly at my mother, who gave a quick nod, stood, and retrieved the pie, doling it out slice by slice, although she seemed to be having some difficulty creating perfect slices.

When my fork tried to make its way through the pie, the problem was evident. In her rush, my mother had somehow chosen the wrong pie pan in which to discard her chicken bones, the one with the pie crust. How she had managed this was unclear, but given the chaos in the kitchen, it could have been anything.

But the fact was, she had served us a Pumpkin Chicken Bone Pie, and it was more than a few minutes before she could bring herself to laugh about it. But she did, we all did, my bother especially because his slice contained the chicken's wishbone, which threw him into a paroxysm of laughter, with the rest of us soon following.

My mother was not finished with her surprises, though. As each of us carefully conducted our archaeological digs into the pie, she pulled out a can of whipped cream — the perfect complement to chicken bones. Before long, we managed to separate the bones from the pie and go through the entire can of whipped cream. Everyone was thoroughly satisfied except my younger brother, who demanded more whipped cream from a can that had already given up its last creamy pffft.

My mother, who was on a roll when it came to surprises, was perhaps too indulgent of my brother's demands. She got up from the table and took the can to the can opener that was bolted to the frame of the kitchen door. She flipped the can over so the nozzle pointed at the floor, and placed the can's bottom in the can opener.

One crank was all that was needed for the third and final surprise, a lesson and cautionary tale in the science of pressure differences and escaping gases. The can erupted explosively, spraying my mother, the walls, the ceiling, and everyone at the table with whipped cream.

Nonplussed, my mother took a blob of cream from her face and stuck it in her mouth. "Works for me," she said.

Lucille Ball would have been proud.

Day 6

HELL-BENT FOR LEATHER

I DON'T KNOW ABOUT YOU, but the Christmas presents I tend to remember are the presents I asked for—begged for, pleaded for, wrote to Santa for, bargained with the devil for—and the presents that came out of left field, wholly unexpected. Such was the case that particular Christmas, when I tromped sleepy eyed into the living room, my eyes growing wide as I parsed out the shape of one particular gift under the tree: a matched set of single-action revolvers, cap guns par excellence, bright chrome exemplars of Old West violence, complete with faux pearl grips and a cowhide double-holstered belt ringed by genuine imitation bullets.

My brother was already there, sitting under the tree, a gun in each hand, on the lookout for savages and pew-pew-pewing away at anything that moved, including me, but not yet realizing that a gift he had not yet opened contained fifty rolls of caps. Minutes later, we buckled up and loaded up, and raced around the house fast and reckless, guns blazing—er, snapping—and hell-bent for leather, intent on protecting our wagon train and bringing Black Bart to justice, dead or alive.

Our rampage did not go unnoticed by my mother, who grabbed both of us by the arms as we raced full-tilt toward the kitchen, where now in the guise of outlaws, we were set to make off with a fresh-baked pie. She disarmed both of us, but promised to return our guns once everyone had a chance to open the rest of the presents under the tree, which usually meant two or perhaps three small gifts, Tinker Toys and the like, useful on a rainy day, but otherwise of no particular interest.

But this year there was an additional gift for me, one that had been wrapped by someone with few skills in wrapping, the tiny package ribbon free and over-taped as if to prevent something from escaping. A message was scrawled on the outside: "To Lenny, from your Uncle Buster."

Just saying the words "Uncle Buster" was enough to make most grown men run for cover, but he had always been good to me, teaching me knife skills with his switchblade, including a game where you splayed the fingers of your hand on a table and the other player stabbed at the space between each finger as rapidly as he could. I wasn't much good at it, but he was. If blood was spilled, it was usually his.

I'm not sure how best to describe him, but the words hulking, menacing, and frightening come to mind. In my memory, he is always in a pair of tight-fitting jeans, with a pack of cigarettes rolled up in his white tee shirt. Believe me, if you saw him once, you'd never forget him, thanks to a triangular indentation in his forehead, the result of being on the receiving end of a flatiron thrown by an ex-girlfriend.

If he ever held a job, I'm not aware of it. The only job I link him to is the job he had pulled the year before with his son, bludgeoning a woman to death with a baseball bat in exchange for a small amount of cash from her husband. My cousin had hanged himself in his cell, and

Uncle Buster had received a life sentence.

I looked with alarm at my mother, who nodded. "He sent it from prison, just for you."

I weighed it in my hands. It wasn't heavy enough to contain the switchblade knife he'd promised to get for me one day, and it didn't make a sound when I shook it.

"Open it."

I tugged at the paper and a small box appeared. Well, it wasn't exactly a real box. It was something Uncle Buster had crafted himself out of a discarded cereal box. Inside was a handmade wallet.

I held it up for all to see.

"Aw, isn't that sweet?" my mother said. Everyone else gawped at it like it was something otherworldly.

It was made of brown leather, or something approaching brown leather, all the pieces held together by red gimp that Uncle Buster had laced somewhat carelessly through pre-punched holes. My name had been burned into the leather, which both delighted me and made me wonder why on earth anyone would let Uncle Buster handle a burning iron with other people around.

I set the wallet aside and grabbed my guns back from my mother, racing outside with my brother, both of us rushing into a world with nothing but promise, cap guns blazing, two desperados on the prowl.

I never received another gift from Uncle Buster. He was killed with a shiv shortly after the New Year, in a dispute over cigarettes with a fellow inmate. His wallet followed soon after, unraveling as quickly as Uncle Buster's life had. I held onto the pieces for some years, keeping them in a cigar box that held my most valuable possessions, mostly pretty rocks and cat's-eye marbles. But even that is gone now, lost to time.

The memory remains, still bright, still treasured, of a man who lived life too fast, too reckless, hell-bent for leather.

Day 7

SANTA IN THE MIDDLE

TWO SCORE AND NONE YEARS AGO, Santa faced the greatest challenge of his career, one more challenging than a billion bites of sugar cookies, more challenging than drinking tankers of milk by the sip, more challenging even than going up and down chimneys when they were there, and up and down chimneys when they weren't there, which might be confusing to you, not being Santa and all, but believe me, that last bit is challenging, but not—I repeat, NOT—as challenging as what happened that Christmas forty years ago.

I was thirty-three, recently divorced—it wasn't easy being Mrs. Claus—and living in an efficiency apartment that looked out on my office building directly across the street, where I worked as a book editor, editing the deadly tomes of college presidents with more ego than writing ability, many of whom referred to commas as "funny little curlicues."

I know, you're thinking, "Santa, a book editor?" Well, what better training for handling the poorly crafted letters Santa has to deal with every year and still be forgiving enough to use the pass-fail system of naughty-nice.

Anyway, my challenge that Christmas Eve seemed simple enough, even enjoyable. I was to host my children, David, age 6, and Lisa, age 8, for the big event. It was going to be fun. I had laid in food and candy, decorated the tree, and hidden away many wrapped gifts I thought they would be certain to enjoy.

Lisa, I felt sure, was losing her belief in me, but David was still entranced by my magic. I wanted to win Lisa back and preserve David's wonder, and that, as it turned out, was my greatest challenge. And it hadn't even occurred to me that it would be any challenge at all.

Until bedtime.

We pulled the cushions off the hide-a-bed, stacked them neatly in a corner, and opened the bed. And that's when I realized I was in trouble. How could I sleep in the same bed with them and still manage to put gifts under the tree, nibble at a cookie, sip at a glass of milk, and return to that same bed undetected?

We watched a little television, and then a little more television, and then, somewhere in the middle of "Miracle on 34th Street," they fell asleep. I waited, and waited, the sound of the street traffic dying away to nothing, the last lights in the office building now dark, the cleaning crews off to their own celebrations.

Silence.

I assessed the situation. Lisa was sleeping on my right, David on my left. Our little Christmas tree was just beyond the foot of the bed, blocking me in that direction. My only choice was to somehow slither from under the covers, climb over the back of the couch, and set to work, all without waking the children. And that was just the half of it. I then had to climb over the back of the couch and re-slither under the covers.

And I did it, all of it, settling back into the bed as the

children slept on till the first rays of sun flooded the apartment.

Now, it's possible that Lisa and David would remember this story differently. They may have watched my slithering contortions with one open eye, suppressing the giggles that would surely have been building in them, and said nothing.

Then again, I'm Santa, and I'm magic. Chimneys? Pah, they're nothing! If you want to see magic at work, try Christmas in an efficiency apartment.

Day 8

MY GUMBALL CHRISTMAS

I WAS GRUMBLING THE WAY all small boys grumble when their mother is dragging them by the hand to yet another store in her search for the perfect Christmas gift for someone else. Mom had tricked me into coming with her with the promise of a chocolate milkshake at Weyland's Drug Store, the kind you can't find these days, whipped up in a tall, stainless steel container attached to a serious, 50 billion rpm Waring Blender, using real ice cream, enough to fill two glasses. If it was done just right, there would be a little lump of ice cream at the bottom that you could slide into your mouth, the ultimate finish to the best drink on the planet.

She had kept her promise, and I had the chocolate moustache to prove it, but now I was faced with being tugged and momhandled from one store to the next in the newest of newest marketing creations/abominations: a strip mall. There was a Safeway at one end and a movie theater at the other end, with many shops in between, including a Pep Boys, a Montgomery Ward catalog store, a hardware store, a hairdresser, a dress shop, a men's store, a jeweler, a tobacco shop, and the Ben Franklin Five and Dime, a treasure trove for all things boy.

And that's where the dragging actually began. I had parked myself in front of a window display at Ben Franklin to wait out a conversation my mother was having with Mrs. Armister, our wealthy neighbor from a few blocks away. As I recall, she was wearing one of those fur capes that included the head of a fox grasping its own hide. As distracting and disturbing as that was, my attention was focused on the poster in the window and an accompanying very large jar of gumballs. Ben Franklin was having a contest. Guess the number of gumballs and you not only got the gumballs, but you also got a ten-minute shopping spree. Anything in the store you could fit into a galvanized mop bucket, you could keep.

My imagination reeled at the possibilities: caps and cap guns, dice, decks of cards, Little Detective handcuffs, toy soldiers, penny candies — candy! I studied the jar intently, putting my hand up to the window to get a rough measurement of its height and width. Then I looked at the gumballs themselves, some red, some green to link the contest to Christmas, and all about the size of my cat's-eye marbles. I counted the number of gumballs in the bottom layer, or at least the ones I could see. Then I counted the number of obvious rows of gumballs from top to bottom. And then I was jerked away from the window by my mother.

I soon discovered that struggling was not an option, and relented, following her calmly, if glumly, from store to store as she shopped for what she called "notions," whatever those were. All the while, my little mind was working the numbers on the gumball contest. How many gumballs would fit in that cylindrical jar? How big were the gumballs, exactly? What was a cylinder, anyway? It seemed both simple and complicated. My biggest fear was that math was somehow involved. In fact, I was certain math was involved, so I took the problem to my sister when we got home.

My sister, Nancy, was five years older and much further along on the death march through the mathematics curriculum. I explained the problem to her, and she in turn gave her shoulders a little shrug and told me to get lost. She was playing with her paper dolls and had reached a particularly dramatic moment involving the fate of Patricia Primbottom and her only male paper doll, Bob the Boozer.

As much as I enjoyed a good dramatic moment, I had needs, mathematical needs, so I grabbed Bob the Boozer and threatened to tear him in half, a fate he certainly deserved, considering his ill treatment of Miss Primbottom, but a fate that horrified Nancy to the point that she agreed to set the dolls aside and introduce me to the concepts of pi, diameters, and the formulas for the volume of cylinders like the jar and spheres like the gumballs.

Equipped with this new knowledge and a few math formulas scrawled on a piece of scrap paper, I set about my task. I won't bother you with the formulas. If you've forgotten them, just Google them for yourself. They probably won't get you any closer to the answer than I got, because as elegant as the formulas were, they only told me two things: the approximate volume occupied by a gumball and the approximate volume of the jar. The real question was not so much how much volume a gumball occupied, but how much volume it DIDN'T occupy when it was stacked in the jar.

My calculations determined that 537 gumballs would

equal the total volume of the jar, so I knew the real number had to be less than that, but how much less? In the end, I just took a stab at it, wrote in 488 on the entry form, along with my name and phone number (Jordan 8650), and dropped the little form into the collection box next to the cash register at Ben Franklin.

And then I waited.

Time seemed to stand as still as the phone in the living room, which refused to ring on the morning of Contest Announcement Day, or at noon of that day, or at dinner time of that day. But then, when all hope was lost and I had resigned myself to a life without gumballs, the phone rang. My mother answered it, and her face brightened almost immediately.

"It's for you," she said, turning to Nancy. "You seem to have won a contest."

Nancy flounced past me, gloating. "Remind me to tell you about stacking theory," she whispered.

I was crushed, flattened, inconsolable, but I was dragged nonetheless to the great event, my sister's ten-minute shopping spree. Her race through the store seemed to go on forever, the crowd cheering her on as she put the ickiest stuff in her bucket: bobby pins, bracelet charms, perfume, paper dolls, a bright purple scarf, and more. It was disgusting.

But like most great and minor disasters, there was a bright side—she absolutely detested gumballs. For weeks after and right through Christmas, my tongue was alternately red or green or that color you get when you mix red and green, which involves color theory, I'm told. If you've forgotten that, there's always Google.

Day 9

THE JUNKMAN'S CHRISTMAS

MY FATHER COLLECTED JUNK. A LOT OF JUNK. If you were thinking of having a yard sale or a garage sale, the first rule of success was to let my father know the date and time, because he would be there, and all those things you thought were worthless, including that ceramic thing with one leg that sort of looked like a giraffe, would be scooped up by my father for display in our home, which the neighbors referred to as "the yard sale that moved indoors." Out of earshot, of course.

One of his greatest finds, to his mind, was a Santa figure about a foot tall. Under its felt and plastic skin rested an evil mechanism that in full battery was designed to proclaim "Ho-Ho-Ho, Merry Christmas!" as it raised its arms to indicate a successful field goal.

He had picked it up at a yard sale hosted by the Armisters, our wealthy, or at least better-off, neighbors, who were all about battery-operated devices, but who exercised one of the privileges of wealth, discarding perfectly good items out of boredom, which they referred to as "ennui."

Of course, this particular Santa was not in perfectly good condition. No, it was more like a severely emotionally disturbed Santa. Instead of saying, "Ho-Ho-Ho, Merry Christmas!" it said, in the best of my ability to interpret, "Ho-Ho-Hotcha" followed by a screeching sound so disturbing it made small children and pets scatter for cover. The sound, accompanied by Santa's fixed, insanely gleeful expression and slowly rising arms, made you feel like some demon from hell was coming for you.

Once my father realized its effect on people, he used it year after year to unmercifully startle and scare people who came by the house at Christmas, particularly my friends. By the third Christmas, most of my friends refused to come into the house without assurances that the Santa was nowhere about.

"Is it?" they would say. Just two words, and I knew exactly what they meant.

"Yes, but my father's taking a nap, so it's safe."

Then they would come in, and there the Santa would be, sitting on the mantle of our fake fireplace. My friends would shudder upon seeing it, and then we'd race to the relative safety of my bedroom, where we would play until it was time for them to go home. Even then, they made me escort them out of the house for fear that the evil beast would jump out at them before they made it to the front door.

My father had weaponized Christmas.

And so it continued, year after year, until that one Christmas when not even fresh batteries could coax it to life. The neighborhood rejoiced at the news, but my father, who was given to dark moods, just sat all day in his chair in front of the television, fiddling with the on-off switch, replacing or jiggling the batteries, checking the wire leads and solder points, and all but performing emergency surgery on his now mute Santa. It could still raise its arms, but without its terrorizing shriek, it was really just a pathetic assemblage of felt and plastic.

The next morning, Santa was nowhere to be found. My father had retreated to his workshop to upholster a client's sofa, and my mother refused to talk about it.

"Let's just say it's gone, okay?"

"But—"

"And whatever you do, never ask your father about it."

And then she had turned back to her work at the sewing machine, which whirred and rumbled all day in my memory as she helped my father by sewing up cushions and sofa skirts and whatever else needed sewing.

The Santa was never seen again. One rumor was that my father had given it to his best friend, Romeo Labona, who had a knack for fixing electrical devices, but once the next Christmas passed without the reappearance of the Santa, we all knew that it would never return to terrorize the neighborhood. America was safe once more.

Even so, even now, I make it a point to steer clear of the Christmas decoration aisles at our local drug store, for fear that I'll come upon a nicely boxed Santa with a "try me" button you push to hear it say, "Ho-Ho-Ho, Merry Christmas!"

I advise you to do the same.

Day 10
ON DAISY'S POND

THE FIRST THING I NOTICE about my sister's Christmas tree is the display under it, which was passed down to her by my Grandma Daisy. It's a mirror, surrounded by spun cotton to create the look of a frozen pond, on which several antique lead figures skate: a young boy in red mittens, his little sister (or so we always imagined) trying to keep up, and a man and woman skating close together arm in arm, young lovers all bright and smiling and having the time of their lives, along with their dog, who stands along the edge of the pond, afraid of the ice but eager to join them, and barking his head off for all eternity.

I pick up the young boy, and I am back in my grandmother's living room, years and years ago, sitting next to her Christmas tree, looking at this very display and surveying the room, which is filled with aunts and uncles and cousins galore. And, of course, there is Grandma Daisy, positioned in a chair in the center of the room, so people could kiss her when they arrive and kiss her when they departed.

In my memory, Grandma Daisy sits there still, anchored to her chair, all but oblivious to the swirl of her children and grandchildren and who all else knows has come willingly or been dragged to the annual Christmas event at "granny's house." She is a small woman, with silver hair done up in tight, tiny curls thanks to a home

permanent kit applied just this morning by her daughter
Bessie, the middle child of her thirteen children, who has
also done her up in a flowered dress more appropriate
for spring, and topped that off with a red Christmas
sweater featuring holly berries and reindeer. Her dress is
not long enough to cover her stockings, which end in
thick rolls just below her knees, revealing skin that is
parchment white.

Bessie has placed her in a chair at the center of the
room, as always, and as Daisy sits there staring blankly
into space with her head and arms resting on freshly
pinned antimacassars, she looks more like a display than
a woman who has endured seventeen pregnancies and a
life in the rough and tumble of near poverty with an
alcoholic husband who took the strap to her when he had
a mind to, despite the efforts of her sons, my father
included, to stop him. But you dare not mention his name
in anger in Daisy's presence. Despite it all, she still
mourns his death, which was as tragic as it was horrific,
the man trapped inside a boiler he was trying to repair,
his body too swollen from the heat to fit back out of the
small entry door before the boiler automatically kicked
in, roasting him alive, his body delivered to her in pieces
the next day.

She does not speak, but she is listening, intently, as her
daughter Ruth, the oldest and her caretaker, opines
nonstop on how her government department has gone to
hell since she retired.

"Nincompoops," she says, jerking her clenched fists up
in front of her chest in a way that suggests she could snap
their necks and think nothing of it.

Daisy blinks her ice-blue eyes, but more out of
boredom than alarm. Ruth is being Ruth, and Daisy just
wants her to stop for once and not natter on and on like
she was Queen of the May, which she thinks she is, no
doubt about that.

I glance around the room. Uncle Ira and Aunt May are
sitting on the couch next to me, along with their
daughter, Dorothy, who is trapped within herself, unable
or unwilling to speak. Beyond them is the long dining
room table, chock-a-block with food and surrounded by
my many aunts and uncles, including my Uncle Fred, the
redheaded uncle, the "milkman's kid," who is red-faced
and pounding the table to make his point in an argument
that arises every Christmas, only the topic changing.

At this point, I usually retreated to Grandma Daisy's
bedroom at the back of the house, where many other
cousins could be found, all in the throes of boredom,
biding their time until their parents had had their fill of
food and conversation, and made their excuses to leave,
most wanting to "make it home before dark," which
would invariably lead to a rapid exit of all but a few
aunts and uncles and their tribes.

Daisy's small four-poster bed wasn't big enough for
more than a few kids, so most of us sat on the floor, some
sitting quietly, others bragging loudly about the treasures
they had received from Santa. I always sat in front of the
small bookshelf next to her bed, which contained the
complete works of Charles Dickens, bound in leather
with gilt-edged pages that smelled of death. I would pull
out a volume and start reading.

"It was the best of times, it was the worst of times, it was the age of wisdom, it was the age of foolishness, it was the epoch of belief, it was the epoch of incredulity, it was the season of Light, it was the season of Darkness. . . ."

I would read more of it to you, but at about this time, my mother would always appear, my coat in her hands, sending a clear message that we were leaving, my father eager to get home before dark. We would make our way back to the living room, lean into the cloud of lavender that surrounded Grandma Daisy, and dutifully peck her on the cheek.

"Do you remember it?" my sister says, startling me.

I smile up at her and put the little skater down on his frozen mirrored pond.

"Oh, yes, especially Uncle Fred."

She rolls her eyes at me. She remembers, too.

Day 11

SANTA TAKES A TUMBLE

MY FATHER TOLD YARNS. BIG ONES. Yarns about fish of impossible dimensions. Yarns about ghosts and leprechauns. If something was impossible, impractical, or downright strange, my father had a yarn for it. So it should have been no surprise to me that he would have a yarn or two to tell about Santa.

I was on the cusp between belief and disbelief, and not quite sure which way I'd fall that particular Christmas. Was there a Santa? It had all seemed so clear the year before, but now as Christmas Eve wore on and we set about trimming the tree with strung popcorn and paper chains, and setting out a plate of fresh-baked sugar cookies for Santa, I was not so sure. I wanted proof — and I had a plan.

"Dad," I asked, "is there really a Santa Claus?"

Dad didn't miss a beat. "Well, of course there's a Santa Claus. Where do you think all the presents come from?"

"Your closet, maybe?"

He was clearly taken aback, but like all tellers of yarns, he was quick to recover. "Oh, those, they're just extras, little somethings. I couldn't possibly afford the gifts that Santa has been bringing you."

I shrugged. "I guess."

He had a point. No one would confuse our humble *Thank God for Duct Tape* existence with, say, our neighbors, the Armisters, who had a real Lionel train chugging around their tree and a new shark-finned Cadillac in the driveway.

"Well, good, I'm glad we had this little talk." He turned and threw a handful of tinsel at the tree, which was now leaning in a way that suggested imminent collapse.

I wasn't about to let him off the hook that easily, though. "But how does he get in here? Our fireplace is fake."

It was true. My father had installed it himself, complete with a stack of fake logs over a crinkled up piece of parchment that rotated under the logs and was backlit by a red, flickering light. It was just pathetic.

"Well, of course he doesn't come down the chimney. We don't have one."

"So how does he get in?"

My father paused only briefly to take a bite of one of Santa's cookies, his lips coming away sugary red. "Why, he just walks in the front door, is all."

He almost had me. It was a time, believe it or not, when people rarely locked their doors, day or night. "So what if we locked the doors tonight? What would he do then?"

My sister, who was five years older and well past the cusp, decided to chime in as a co-conspirator from her perch atop the back of the living room couch. "Don't be silly. Santa can just walk through walls."

My father could have taken the easy way out and agreed with her, but he saw the look of incredulity on my face and decided to take a more yarn-worthy tack. "Oh, some believe that, that's true, but I think if we locked the door tonight, he'd know — he'd know in the way he knows who's naughty and who's nice — and he'd just leave the presents on the roof."

My sister gasped. "Or just outside the front door," she said quickly, sensing well before my father where this conversation was headed.

"Oh, no," said my father. "He's much too busy for that. No, I'm sure he'd leave the presents on the roof, call out, 'On Dasher, on Blitzkrieg' and so forth, and fly away."

My trap was set.

"Oh, really?" I said, standing and walking to the door, locking it with a tad too much bravado for a boy in Daffy Duck footie pajamas. "Good night, then."

I strutted from the room, down the hall to my room, and closed the door. A brief, though muffled, conversation then ensued between my father and my sister. I couldn't make out what they were saying, but I did hear my mother walk into the room and say something that sounded like scolding. But then, just moments later, they all laughed.

And then all was quiet. I listened as hard as I could, and tried to stay awake, but sleep overtook me.

The ambulance arrived a few hours later, lights flashing, siren blaring, awakening me with a start. I raced from my room, down the hall, into the living room, and out the open front door, where I saw my father being lifted onto a stretcher, my mother and sister hovering over him, surrounded by what must have been the entire neighborhood. Even the Armisters were there in their matching bathrobes.

"What happened?" I shouted.

"Quiet," said my sister. "Dad fell off the roof."

"But—"

"Don't worry," said my mother. "He was just helping Santa, and he slipped. He'll be fine."

I turned and looked back at the roof of the house. A red wagon was straddling its peak, and other presents, wrapped and unwrapped, were scattered from the peak to the eaves and on the ground below. It looked like an avalanche of presents.

My father, not one to ignore the opportunity of a crowd, beckoned me to his side and, through gritted teeth and the pain of a broken leg, announced for all to hear what would become a neighborhood legend and the reason many children continued to believe in Santa for years.

"I was just helping Santa with the presents, and slipped when he and his reindeer flew away. Surely you saw it. I mean, Rudolph's nose is as bright as the ambulance's lights."

Some adults and older kids laughed, and a few even clapped, but we children on the cusp just turned and gaped at the wagon on the roof, our Christmas beacon. And then, as if by signal, little Bobby Armister shouted, "Presents!" and everyone scattered, each running for home and the treasures that awaited them.

I think if my father, the Great Embellisher, were telling this yarn, right about now he'd throw in a large group of carolers in turn-of-the-century garb, all holding candles and singing your favorite carol, whatever it might be — you know, the one that brings tears to your eyes and joy to your heart and makes you remember your very best Christmas *ever*.

But to me, the idea of carolers showing up at 3:00 a.m. is kind of disturbing, so I'll just end this tale with what we kids imagined that Santa must have said as his sleigh lifted into the air and my father's eyes grew wide as he began his tumble: "Merry Christmas to all, and to all a good night!"

A CHRISTMAS BICYCLE

OUR BICYCLES BEGAN TO PICK UP SPEED as we raced down the hill, Tony on the left of me, Luigi on the right, all of us cranking hard at the pedals, each determined to reach the bottom first. I glanced quickly at Tony, who was looking back at me, bug-eyed. . .

My eyes had gone bug-eyed earlier in the day, when I had trudged slowly down the stairs from my bedroom, not expecting much in the way of Christmas presents. It had been a bad year for my father's one-man upholstery business, one of many, so the last thing I was expecting was what I had actually asked for: a bicycle!

It wasn't new, but it was in pretty good shape for an old Raleigh English Racer. The 3-speed gears worked, the brakes seemed okay, and the leather seat was like new. There were scratches, of course, but the maroon paint still gleamed, as did the stainless steel air pump on the diagonal frame bar. It even had a little leather satchel attached to the back of the seat, which I soon found held a few rusted wrenches and a Pep Boys inner tube repair kit that had apparently never been used.

The only thing that looked odd about the bike was the fenders, which were made of an off-white fiberglass rather than metal. I guess the idea was to lighten the bike, making it marginally faster, which I hoped would help me win a race or two with my friends.

There were no other presents for me, other than a few

pieces of candy in my stocking, so I quickly got dressed, threw a couple of grape sodas and quickly prepared peanut butter sandwiches into the satchel, and headed out to give my new bike an all-day try. That's when I discovered that Tony and Luigi had each received brand new bikes for Christmas, both of them remarking how sad my bike looked compared to theirs, which had heavily chromed fenders, headlights, horns, and plastic tassels streaming from the hand grips.

Of course, what they didn't have was multiple speeds like my bike. Theirs were traditional American one-speed bikes, with rear-only brakes activated by slamming back on the pedals — useful for leaving skid marks, but not as refined as the front and rear caliper brakes of my English racer. I didn't think they'd stand a chance against me, so the game was on! First one to the bottom of the "R" Street hill, the steepest hill around, would reap a shiny quarter from the other two, enough to pay for the new Burt Lancaster movie that had just opened, with a bag of popcorn to boot.

If I had thought about it, I would have unloaded the satchel, which because of the sodas, had drooped down to rest heavily on the fender, causing it to scrape lightly against the rear tire from time to time. But there just wasn't time. The race was on!

We positioned our bikes in the road, using the rear bumper of my father's old Plymouth as the starting line. The finish line was already a given — the horizontal bump in the road at the bottom of the hill, which marked the path of the underlying culvert that allowed our little creek to flow by. On a snowy day, the bump would have signified that you had made it down the hill alive on your sled. Despite our wishes, there had been no snow the night before, so the hill lay before us, steep and dry.

After some discussion about how to start the race fairly, Steven just started a countdown from three to one, and we were off, Steven taking the early lead as I fumbled to switch gears from first to second. By the fifth or sixth revolution of my bike's wheels, I had made it into third gear and began to steadily close the gap, my speed building quickly, houses and trees beginning to blur, my cheeks beginning to flutter the way the cheeks of test pilots fluttered in a centrifuge.

We were all going fast — too fast. If we had had any sense at all, we would have stopped pedaling and just coasted down the hill, but fifty cents was fifty cents, so we kept pedaling, the bottom of the hill quickly approaching as we raced side by side, the lead going back and forth.

That's when I had glanced at Tony and seen the bug-eyed look he was giving me.

"Fire!" he shouted at me, pointing behind me. "You're on fire!"

I turned my head to take a look, and sure enough, the back of my bicycle was ablaze, flames and smoke billowing from the satchel and the fiberglass fender.

I slammed on the brakes. Unfortunately, I applied more pressure to the front brake than the rear brake, so the bike flipped into the air, tumbling forward, me and the bike parting company during the second revolution, the bike crashing in flames to the ground as I bounced once and splashed into the creek, the water dousing the fire I hadn't known about, on my winter coat, which continued to smoke for some minutes as I slowly stood and checked for broken bones.

Tony helped me out of the creek and up the bank to the road, where we found Luigi already enjoying the rights of salvage, sipping at the one grape soda that had survived the wreck. Flames continued to lick at the satchel and the fender, which had melted onto the road.

"That was something," he said.

If it had been a different era, we would have stood there shaking our heads, going through every possible inflection of "dude." But it was the 1950s, so we just stood there shaking our heads.

"She-it," said Tony, looking down at the twisted wreckage. The handlebars were twisted around, the frame was bent, and neither wheel would ever make a circle again.

"It's not so bad," I said, swatting out the remaining flames with my cap and lifting the bike up, tugging at the handle bars to get them going in the right direction.

"You'll need new wheels," said Luigi.

"And a new frame," said Tony.

I nodded, recognizing what I was pushing back up the hill: a dead bicycle.

Years later, after my mother's death, I was sorting through the contents of the house. I found the bicycle where I had left it that Christmas morning — in the basement, propped up against a wall, a little piece of Christmas ribbon still attached to its handlebars.

I remembered the look on my mother's face that morning as I had dropped the twisted bicycle at her feet, and she had pulled me close, still smelling of Christmas cookies, trying her best to console me. There was sadness, and compassion, and the knowing look of a woman who knew, as I did, that there would be no replacement, no repairs. Christmas would have to wait another year, and there would never be another bicycle under the tree.

I looked down at the bike and gave the front brake lever one last squeeze, a smile growing on my face. I thought then as I think now: we are all memories.

About the Author

Len Boswell was born in a hospital that has since been torn down, grew up on a street that has since changed its name, in a house that has since changed its number. Everywhere around him his life seems to be erasing itself, which is more than a good reason to write down these brief memories of Christmases past. An award-winning writer, he now spends his days in the mountains of West Virginia, with his wife, Ruth, and their two dogs, Shadow and Cinder.

Made in the USA
Columbia, SC
02 December 2017